Preparation for Confirmation

ACCORDING TO THE BALTIMORE CATECHISM

ANGELUS PRESS
2918 TRACY AVENUE, KANSAS CITY, MISSOURI 64109

ANGELUS PRESS

2918 TRACY AVENUE
KANSAS CITY, MISSOURI 64109
PHONE (816) 753-3150
FAX (816) 753-3557
ORDER LINE 1-800-966-7337

ISBN 0-935952-34- 9
First Printing—February 1996

Printed in the United States of America

PART ONE

MINIMUM KNOWLEDGE NECESSARY FOR THE RECEPTION OF CONFIRMATION

(Part One is to be Memorized)

I. PRAYERS

THE SIGN OF THE CROSS

In the Name of the Father and of the Son and of the Holy Ghost. Amen.

THE LORD'S PRAYER

Our Father, Who art in Heaven, hallowed be Thy name, Thy kingdom come; Thy will be done on earth as it is in Heaven. Give us this day our daily bread; and forgive us our trespasses as we forgive those who trespass against us; and lead us not into temptation, but deliver us from evil. Amen.

THE ANGELIC SALUTATION

Hail Mary, full of grace! The Lord is with thee; blessed art thou amongst women and blessed is the fruit of thy womb, Jesus. Holy Mary, Mother of God, pray for us sinners, now and at the hour of our death. Amen.

THE APOSTLES' CREED

I believe in God, the Father Almighty, Creator of Heaven and earth; and in Jesus Christ, His only Son, our Lord; Who was conceived by the Holy Ghost, born of the Virgin Mary, suffered under Pontius Pilate, was crucified, died and was buried. He descended into hell; the third day He arose again from the dead. He ascended into Heaven, sitteth at the right hand of God, the Father Almighty; from thence He shall come to judge the living and the dead. I believe in the Holy Ghost, the Holy Catholic Church, the communion of saints, the forgiveness of sins, the resurrection of the body and life everlasting. Amen.

THE CONFITEOR

I confess to Almighty God, to blessed Mary, ever Virgin, to blessed Michael the Archangel, to blessed John the Baptist, to the holy Apostles Peter and Paul, and to all the saints, that I have sinned exceedingly in thought, word and deed, through my fault, through my fault, through my most grievous fault.

Therefore I beseech blessed Mary, ever Virgin, blessed Michael the Archangel, blessed John the Baptist, the holy Apostles Peter and Paul, and all the saints, to pray to the Lord our God for me.

May the Almighty God have mercy on me, forgive me my sins and bring me to life everlasting. Amen.

May the Almighty and Merciful Lord grant me pardon, absolution and remission of all my sins. Amen.

THE ACTS OF FAITH, HOPE, CHARITY, & CONTRITION

The Act of Faith

O my God, I firmly believe that Thou art one God in three Divine Persons; Father, Son and Holy Ghost. I believe that Thy Divine Son became man and died for our sins, and that He will come to judge the living and the dead. I believe these and all the truths which the Holy Catholic Church teaches, because Thou hast revealed them Who canst neither deceive nor be deceived.

The Act of Hope

O my God, relying on Thine infinite goodness and promises, I hope to obtain pardon of my sins, the help of Thy grace and life everlasting, through the merits of Jesus Christ, my Lord and Redeemer.

The Act of Charity

O my God, I love Thee above all things, with my whole heart and soul, because Thou art all good and worthy of all my love. I love my neighbor as myself for the love of Thee. I forgive all who have injured me and ask pardon of all whom I have injured.

The Act of Contrition

O my God, I am heartily sorry for having offended Thee, and I detest all my sins, because I dread the loss of heaven and the pains of hell, but most of all because they offend Thee, my God Who art all good and deserving of all my love. I firmly resolve, with the help of Thy grace to confess my sins, to do penance, and to amend my life. Amen.

II. THE LAWS OF GOD AND THE CHURCH

1. *What are the ten commandments?*

(1) I am the Lord, thy God; thou shalt not have strange gods before me.

(2) Thou shalt not take the name of the Lord thy God in vain.

(3) Remember thou keep holy the Sabbath day.

(4) Honor thy father and thy mother.

(5) Thou shalt not kill.

(6) Thou shalt not commit adultery.

(7) Thou shalt not steal.

(8) Thou shalt not bear false witness against thy neighbor.

(9) Thou shalt not covet thy neighbor's wife.

(10) Thou shalt not covet thy neighbor's goods.

2. *What are the precepts of the Church?*

(1) To hear Mass on Sundays and holy days of obligation.

(2) To fast and abstain on the days appointed.

(3) To confess our sins at least once a year.

(4) To receive Holy Communion during Easter time.

(5) To contribute to the support of the Church.

(6) To observe the laws of the Church concerning marriage.

3. Which are the Holy Days of Obligation
(1) Three Feasts of our Lord:
Christmas Day, December 25th
Circumcision, January 1st
Ascension Thursday, 40 days after Easter

(2) Two Feasts of our Lady:
The Assumption of the Blessed Virgin, August 15th
The Immaculate Conception, December 8th

(3) One Feast of the Saints:
All Saints Day, November 1st.

In Canada, the Feast of *Epiphany*, January 6th is observed instead of the Feast of the *Assumption*, August 15th.

III. THE SEVEN SACRAMENTS

1. What are the seven sacraments?
(1) Baptism
(2) Confirmation
(3) Holy Eucharist
(4) Penance
(5) Extreme Unction
(6) Holy Orders
(7) Matrimony

2. What is Baptism?
Baptism is the sacrament which cleanses us from original sin, makes us Christians, children of God and heirs of Heaven.

3. What is Confirmation?
Confirmation is the sacrament through which the Holy Ghost comes to us in a special way and enables us to profess our Faith as strong and perfect Christians and soldiers of Jesus Christ.

4. What is the Holy Eucharist?
Holy Eucharist is the sacrament which contains the Body and Blood, Soul and Divinity of our Lord Jesus Christ, under the appearances of bread and wine.

5. What is Penance?

Penance is the sacrament by which sins committed after Baptism are forgiven through the absolution of the priest.

6. What is Extreme Unction?

Extreme Unction is the sacrament which, through the anointing and prayer of the priest, gives health and strength to the soul, and sometimes to the body, when we are in danger of death from sickness, accident or old age.

7. What is Holy Orders?

Holy Orders is the sacrament by which bishops, priests and other ministers of the Church are ordained and receive the power and grace to perform their sacred duties.

8. What is Matrimony?

Matrimony is the sacrament which unites a Christian man and woman in lawful marriage.

IV. THE EFFECTS OF CONFIRMATION

1. What are the effects of Confirmation?

The principal effects of Confirmation are:

(1) An increase of sanctifying grace received in Baptism.

(2) The strengthening of our faith.

(3) The gifts of the Holy Ghost.

(4) An indelible mark imprinted on our souls.

2. What are the seven gifts of the Holy Ghost?

Wisdom, Understanding, Counsel, Fortitude, Knowledge, Piety and Fear of the Lord.

3. Explain the purpose of the various gifts of the Holy Ghost.

(1) **Wisdom** gives us a relish for the things of God and directs our whole life and all our actions to His honor and glory.

(2) **Understanding** enables us to know more clearly the mysteries of faith.

(3) **Counsel** warns us of the deceits of the devil and of the dangers to salvation.

(4) **Fortitude** strengthens us to do the will of God in all things.

(5) **Knowledge** enables us to discover the will of God in all things.

(6) **Piety** makes us love God as a Father and obey Him because we love Him.

(7) **Fear of the Lord** fills us with a dread of sin.

V. THE DOCTRINE OF THE TRINITY

1. Is there only one God?
Yes, there is only one God.

2. How many Persons are there in God?
In God there are three Divine Persons: the Father, the Son and the Holy Ghost.

3. Is the Father God?
Yes, the Father is God and the First Person of the Blessed Trinity.

4. Is the Son God?
Yes, the Son is God and the Second Person of the Blessed Trinity.

5. Is the Holy Ghost God? Yes, the Holy Ghost is God and the Third Person of the Blessed Trinity.

6. What do we mean by the Blessed Trinity?
By the Blessed Trinity we mean one and the same God in three Divine Persons.

7. Are the Three Divine Persons really distinct from one another?
The Three Divine Persons are really distinct from one another.

8. Are the Three Divine Persons perfectly equal to one another?
The Three Divine Persons are perfectly equal to one another, because all are one and the same God.

9. How are the Three Divine Persons, though really distinct from one another, one and the same God?
The Three Divine Persons, though really distinct from one another are one and the same God because all three have the same divine nature.

10. Can we fully understand how the Three Divine Persons,

though really distinct from one another, are one and the same God?

We cannot understand how the Three Divine Persons, though really distinct from one another, are one and the same God, because this is a supernatural mystery.

VI. THE INCARNATION AND REDEMPTION

1. Did God abandon man after Adam fell into sin?

God did not abandon man after Adam fell into sin, but promised to send into the world a Savior to free man from his sins and to reopen the gates of heaven.

2. Who is the Savior of all men?

The Savior of all men is Jesus Christ.

3. What is the chief teaching of the Catholic Church about Jesus Christ?

The chief teaching of the Catholic Church about Jesus Christ is that He is God made man.

4. Why is Jesus Christ God?

Jesus Christ is God because He is the only Son of God, having the same divine nature as His Father.

5. Why is Jesus Christ man?

Jesus Christ is man because He is the Son of the Blessed Virgin Mary and has a body and soul like ours.

6. Is Jesus Christ more than one person?

No, Jesus Christ is only one person; and that person is the second Person of the Blessed Trinity.

7. How many natures has Jesus Christ?

Jesus Christ has two natures; the nature of God and the nature of man.

8. Was the Son of God always man?

The Son of God was not always man, but became man at the time of the Incarnation.

9. What is meant by the Incarnation?

By the Incarnation is meant that the Son of God, retaining His divine nature, took to Himself a human nature, that is, a body and soul like ours.

10. How was the Son of God made man?

The Son of God was conceived and made man by the power of the Holy Ghost in the womb of the Blessed Virgin Mary.

11. When was the Son of God conceived and made man?

The Son of God was conceived and made man on Annunciation Day, the day on which the Angel Gabriel announced to the Blessed Virgin Mary that she was to be the Mother of God.

12. Is Saint Joseph the father of Jesus Christ?

Jesus Christ has no human father, but Saint Joseph was the spouse of the Blessed Virgin Mary and the guardian, or foster father, of Jesus Christ.

13. When was Christ born?

Christ was born of the Blessed Virgin Mary on Christmas Day in Bethlehem more than nineteen hundred years ago.

14. What is a supernatural mystery?

A supernatural mystery is a truth which we cannot fully understand, but which we firmly believe because we have God's word for it.

15. What is meant by the Redemption?

By the Redemption is meant that Jesus Christ, as the Redeemer of the whole human race, offered His sufferings and death to God as a fitting sacrifice in satisfaction for the sins of men and regained for them the right to be children of God and heirs of heaven.

PART TWO

THE SACRAMENT OF CONFIRMATION

(It is not necessary to memorize Part Two, but it must be thoroughly understood)

I. DIVINE INSTITUTION OF CONFIRMATION

1. When was Confirmation instituted?

The exact time at which Confirmation was instituted is not known. It is certain that Christ instituted this sacrament and instructed His Apostles in its use at some time before His Ascension into heaven.

2. What promise did Christ make before He left this earth?

He promised the guidance of the Holy Ghost, the Third Person of the Trinity, the "Spirit of Truth" Whom He would send to teach them all things whatsoever He had told them. "I will ask the Father, and He shall give you another Paraclete, that He may abide with you forever" (John 14:16). "You shall receive the power of the Holy Ghost coming upon you" (Acts 1:8).

3. Did our Lord keep His promise?

Yes, ten days after His Ascension He sent the Holy Ghost down upon the Apostles in the form of tongues of fire. "Suddenly there came a sound from heaven, as of a mighty wind coming, and it filled the whole house where they were sitting. And there appeared to them parted tongues as it were of fire, and it sat upon every one of them. And they were filled with the Holy Ghost; and they began to speak with divers tongues according as the Holy Ghost gave them to speak" (Acts 2:2).

4. What effects did the descent of the Holy Ghost have upon the Apostles?

The Apostles were truly confirmed, that is to say, *strengthened;* their *understanding* was fully penetrated with the whole and entire doctrine of Divine Faith; their *minds* clearly grasped the Divine truths; their *will* was entirely under His sway so that they fearlessly preached the Gospel to the whole world.

5. What effects did the descent of the Holy Ghost have upon the early Christians?

They received a special assistance to enable them to undergo great afflictions and severe trials on account of their new faith.

6. What commission did our Lord give the Apostles?

He commanded them to confer the Holy Ghost by the imposition of hands on all who were properly disposed to receive the sacrament of Confirmation. "As the Father hath sent Me, I also send you" (John 20:21).

7. Does the Church still practice the ancient custom of imposing hands to call down the Holy Ghost upon those who have been baptized?

Yes, the Church still possesses and dispenses the graces of the Holy Ghost in a special sacrament by the imposition of hands through the ministry of the bishops to the faithful after Baptism.

II. NATURE OF CONFIRMATION

1. What is Confirmation?

Confirmation is a sacrament of the New Law, instituted by our Lord Jesus Christ, which strengthens the divine life in us, and gives to those who are baptized the Holy Ghost with all His gifts.

2. Why is it called Confirmation?

Because this sacrament *strengthens* and perfects the new life which the grace of Jesus Christ bestows in Baptism.

3. What are some of the names given by the Fathers of the

Church to the sacrament of Confirmation?
(1) Imposition of hands.
(2) The Sacrament of Holy Chrism.
(3) The Seal of our Lord.
(4) The Spiritual Seal.
(5) The Sign by which the Holy Ghost is received.

4. Why is Confirmation a true sacrament?
Because it has all the conditions that are required for a sacrament.
(1) An outward sign.
(2) An inward grace.
(3) The institution by Jesus Christ.

5. What is the outward sign of Confirmation?
It is the visible action by which the sacrament is administered, and consists of matter and form, which signify the grace to be conferred.

6. What are the matter and form of Confirmation?
(1) The *matter* of the sacrament consists in the laying on of the bishop's hands, and the anointing with chrism.

(2) The *form* consists in the sacred words pronounced by the bishop, which express the receiving of the Holy Ghost and the sealing of the soul in Jesus Christ.

7. What is Holy Chrism? What does the oil signify?
(1) The Holy Chrism is composed of olive oil and fragrant balsam blessed by the bishop on Holy Thursday.

(2) The oil signifies the inward strength conferred upon the soul by the Holy Ghost.

8. What does the balsam mixed with oil signify?
Balsam is mixed with oil when it is consecrated by the bishop to signify that he who is to be confirmed receives the grace to keep himself free from sinful corruption and to send forth the sweet odor of a holy life.

9. What does the bishop say when he consecrates the chrism?
"God grant this virtue to the chrism of the Holy Ghost, that by the sanctification infused by chrism, the corruption of the first birth

may be absorbed, the holy temple of each one may breathe the lovely odor of an innocent life."

10. Is Confirmation necessary for salvation?

Confirmation is not, like Baptism, absolutely necessary for salvation. But all Catholics ought to receive it if they have the opportunity, as it confers sacramental grace.

11. Is it a sin to neglect Confirmation?

It is a sin to neglect Confirmation, especially in these evil days when faith and morals are exposed to so many and such violent temptations.

III. THE MINISTER OF CONFIRMATION

1. Who has the power to confirm?

The power to confirm resides in the bishops of the Church who, succeeding the Apostles, are the *ordinary* ministers of Confirmation.

2. Who is the extraordinary minister of Confirmation?

The *extraordinary* minister of Confirmation is a priest who has received the power by special delegation of the Apostolic See.*

(*By a decree of September 14, 1946, the Pastor in his own territory may confirm all the faithful who are in danger of death from a serious illness from which it is foreseen they will die.)

3. Can the extraordinary minister consecrate the chrism used in Confirmation.

No, he must use the chrism which has been consecrated by the bishop.

4. What must an extraordinary minister do before conferring Confirmation?

He must announce beforehand that while a bishop is the ordinary minister, he himself has a special power from the Holy See to confer the sacrament; and he must use the same rite as the bishop.

5. When may Confirmation be administered?

Confirmation may be administered at any time of the year, at any hour, even in the evening if the bishop should so arrange.

6. *Where does the bishop confirm?*

The proper place of the ceremony is in the Church, but the bishop, for a reasonable cause, may confer the sacrament in any becoming place.

IV. DISPOSITIONS FOR CONFIRMATION

1. *Who can be confirmed?*

Anyone who has been baptized but not yet confirmed can receive this sacrament.

2. *Has the Church ever confirmed infants?*

Yes, in the early days of Christianity and even now in certain Eastern countries, the Church confirms infants immediately after Baptism.

3. *At what age is Confirmation usually administered?*

In most parts of the Church at the present day only those who have attained the use of reason are admitted to Confirmation.

4. *What are the conditions required for receiving Confirmation?*

(1) The person must be a baptized Catholic.

(2) He should be in the state of grace; that is, free from all mortal sin.

(3) He should take a saint's name, one different from his baptismal name.

(4) He should be well-instructed in the principal doctrines of his Faith.

5. *What knowledge should a person have who is to be confirmed?*

He should know the *Lord's Prayer*, the *Angelic Salutation*, the *Apostles' Creed*, the Commandments of God, the Precepts of the Church, the doctrine of the sacraments, especially the nature and effects of the sacrament of Confirmation.

6. *What should be the dispositions of the soul of the person to be confirmed?*

He should make a worthy confession and spend some time in recollection so as to be prepared to receive the Holy Ghost with His sevenfold gifts.

7. Must the sacrament of Confirmation be received fasting?

No, today candidates for Confirmation are not required to be fasting.

8. What would happen should a person present himself to receive Confirmation knowing himself to be in the state of mortal sin?

He would commit a grave sin of sacrilege and while the sacrament would be received, he would not receive its graces until he made a good confession and received absolution.

V. THE CEREMONIES OF CONFIRMATION

1. How is Confirmation administered?

(1) The bishop about to confirm, with his hand extended toward those to be confirmed, prays that the Holy Ghost descend upon them with His sevenfold gifts.

(2) He *lays his hand* upon each one, *anointing* him with holy chrism on the forehead by the sign of the Cross and pronouncing the *sacramental words*.

(3) He gently *strikes* each one on the cheek, and finally gives all who have been confirmed his *blessing*.

2. Why is the forehead anointed with the sign of the Cross?

(1) To teach us that sacramental grace is given in virtue of the sacrifice of the Cross only.

(2) To remind those confirmed that they must not be ashamed to profess boldly their faith in Christ Jesus crucified.

(3) That by this sacred unction the soul is sealed in the Holy Ghost with a spiritual, indelible mark, which enrolls those confirmed forever in the service of Christ.

3. What does the bishop say in anointing the person he confirms?

He says: "I sign thee with the sign of the Cross, and I confirm thee with the chrism of salvation, in the name of the Father, and of the Son and of the Holy Ghost."

4. What does the bishop say when he gives the blow on the

cheek of those confirmed?
He says: "Peace be to you."

5. *What does the blow on the cheek signify?*
It reminds them that by Confirmation they were strengthened to suffer; and if necessary, even to die for Christ.

6. *How should the candidates present themselves for Confirmation?*
(1) They should appear in decent or modest dress.
(2) They should have their foreheads neat, and their hair so arranged as to leave the forehead free to be anointed.
(3) They should approach the altar with due reverence and with hands joined before their breast.

7. *What do we hand the bishop's assistant as we kneel to receive the sacrament?*
We hand him a small card which contains the name of the patron saint chosen at Confirmation; also the baptismal and family name and the name of the sponsor.

8. *What should candidates do when about to be confirmed?*
(1) They should most fervently ask for the gifts of the Holy Ghost.
(2) They should promise to live and die as loyal and faithful soldiers of Christ.
(3) They should be present from the beginning of the sacred rite and remain until the bishop has given the benediction.

9. *Why is a new name taken in Confirmation?*
The candidate for Confirmation takes another name to the one received in Baptism to remind him:
(1) That he is to place himself under the protection of another patron saint, whom he chooses as his advocate before God;
(2) that he is to follow the exemplary life of the new patron, remaining steadfast until death.

10. *What penance does the Bishop give to those he has confirmed?*
He tells them to say the *Apostles' Creed*, the *Our Father* and the *Hail Mary* as a penance.

VI. SPONSORS AND PARENTS

1. Why are sponsors taken in Confirmation?
Sponsors in Confirmation, like those in Baptism, present the candidates to the bishop and undertake to see that the child is brought up in the Catholic Faith and in the practice of his religion.

2. What is required of sponsors in Confirmation?
(1) They must be practicing Catholics.

(2) They must have been confirmed and able to fulfill their duties as spiritual guardians.

(3) They must be different from the baptismal sponsors.

3. How many sponsors are necessary?
There should be one sponsor for each candidate, a godfather for boys and a godmother for girls.

4. May one or two sponsors stand for all the candidates?
When it is altogether impossible for the candidates to have each his own sponsor, at least two men shall act as sponsors for the boys and two women as sponsors for the girls.

5. Who chooses the sponsor?
The sponsor is chosen by the candidate or by his parents or guardians; otherwise by the bishop or parish priest.

6. What are the duties of sponsors during Confirmation?
(1) They should accompany the candidates and present them to the bishop at the altar.

(2) While the candidate is being confirmed, they should physically touch his shoulder with their right hand, standing immediately behind him.

7. What are the duties of sponsors after Confirmation?
They should take a permanent interest in their spiritual children and should see that they receive a Christian education whenever the parents fail in this duty.

8. Does the sponsor contract a spiritual relationship?
Sponsors contract a spiritual relationship with the persons for whom they stood, but this is no longer an impediment to marriage.

9. May clerics or members of religious orders act as sponsors?

No, this is forbidden without special permission.

10. What are the duties of parents whose children are to be confirmed?

(1) They should not neglect to have their children receive the sacrament at the proper time.

(2) They must send them regularly to the preparatory instructions.

(3) They should assist them in order to make a good confession before receiving Confirmation.

(4) After Confirmation they must insist that their children receive the sacraments of Penance and of Holy Eucharist frequently.

11. What are the duties of the confirmed?

Those who have been confirmed should:

(1) Thank God the Holy Ghost for the graces bestowed upon the soul.

(2) Promise steadfastly to profess their Faith and live up to it.

(3) Celebrate the anniversary day of Confirmation.

PART THREE

THE RITE OF CONFIRMATION
AND PREPARATORY PRAYERS

I. PRAYERS BEFORE CONFIRMATION

*Prayer for Obtaining a Right Disposition
for Receiving the Sacrament of Confirmation*

O my God, through Thy great mercy, I have received three of Thy most holy sacraments; the first to make me Thy child, the second to efface the stains which sin had made in my soul, the third to unite me with Thy Divine Son. Grant, then, I beseech Thee, that the sacrament which I am now preparing to receive, may avail to make me a perfect Christian; that it may give me strength and courage to combat my evil habits, to overcome all my temptations, to conform myself perfectly to Thy law, and to become a true soldier of Jesus Christ, ready to suffer anything rather than renounce His holy religion, and to maintain it, if need be, even at the peril of my life. This I most earnestly beseech Thee, O my God, through the merits of Thy Son our Lord, Who liveth and reigneth with Thee forever and ever. Amen.

Prayer for the Seven Gifts of the Holy Ghost

O Almighty and eternal God, Thou hast vouchsafed to adopt me for Thy child in the holy sacrament of Baptism; Thou hast granted me the remission of my sins at the tribunal of penance; Thou hast made me to sit at Thy holy table and hast fed me with the Bread of Angels; perfect in me, I beseech Thee, all these benefits. Grant unto me the spirit of Wisdom, that I may despise the

Part III: The Rite of Confirmation and Preparatory Prayers

perishable things of this world, and love the things that are eternal; the spirit of Understanding, to enlighten me and to give the knowledge of religion; the spirit of Counsel, that I may diligently seek the surest ways of pleasing God and obtaining heaven; the spirit of Fortitude, that I may overcome with courage all the obstacles that oppose my salvation; the spirit of Knowledge that I may be enlightened in the ways of God; the spirit of Piety, that I may find the service of God both sweet and amiable; the spirit of Fear, that I may be filled with a loving reverence toward God, and may dread in any way to displease Him. Seal me, in Thy mercy, with the seal of a disciple of Jesus Christ, unto everlasting life; and grant that, carrying the Cross upon my forehead, I may carry it also in my heart, and confessing Thee boldly before me, may merit to be one day reckoned in the number of Thy elect. Amen.

Prayer for the Twelve Fruits of the Holy Ghost

O Holy Spirit, Eternal Love of the Father and the Son, vouchsafe to grant unto me, I beseech Thee, the fruit of Charity, that I may be united to Thee by divine love; the fruit of Joy, that I may be filled with a holy consolation; the fruit of Peace, that I may enjoy inward tranquility of soul; the fruit of Patience, that I may endure humbly everything that may be opposed to my own desires; the fruit of Benignity, that I may willingly relieve the necessities of my neighbor; the fruit of Goodness, that I may be benevolent toward all; the fruit of Longanimity, that I may not be discouraged by delay, but may persevere in prayer; the fruit of Mildness, that I may subdue every rising of evil temper, stifle every murmur, and repress the susceptibilities of my nature in all my dealings with my neighbor; the fruit of Fidelity, that I may rely, with assured confidence, on the word of God; the fruit of Modesty, that I may order my exterior regularly; the fruits of Continency and Chastity, that I may keep my body in such holiness as becometh Thy temple, so that, having, by Thy assistance, preserved my heart pure on earth, I may merit, in Jesus Christ, according to the words of the Gospel, to see God eternally in the glory of His Kingdom. Amen.

An Act of Faith

O Holy Spirit, I firmly believe that I am about to receive Thee in the sacrament of Confirmation. I believe it because Thou hast said it and Thou art the Truth itself.

An Act of Hope

Relying on Thy infinite goodness, O Holy and Sanctifying Spirit, I confidently hope that, receiving Thee in the sacrament of Confirmation, I shall receive the abundance of Thy graces. I trust in Thee that Thou wilt make me a perfect Christian, and that Thou wilt give me strength to confess the Faith, even at the peril of my life.

An Act of Charity

I love Thee, O Holy Spirit, with all my heart, and with all my soul, above all things, because Thou art infinitely good and worthy to be loved. Kindle in my heart the fire of Thy love; and grant that, having received Thee in the sacrament of Confirmation, I may faithfully perform all the duties of my state, to the end of my life.

A Prayer Before Confirmation

O God of infinite goodness, receive, I beseech Thee, my most humble and hearty thanks, for all the favors which Thou hast bestowed upon me, from the very moment of my birth; particularly for that Thou hast been pleased to rank me among those who are now about to be set apart and consecrated to Thee by the sacrament of Confirmation. Thou offerest me the greatest of Thy gifts; Thou art about to seal my soul with the sacred character of a soldier of Jesus Christ, and to send Thy Holy Spirit down upon me, that He may abide within me continually. O my good and merciful Father, encouraged by such special marks of predilection, I venture to implore, with humble confidence, that Thou wouldst Thyself infuse into my heart all the dispositions necessary for its becoming the habitation of such a guest. Alas! O my God, I am far from possessing those sentiments of faith, love, humility and fervor which ought now to animate my soul; but all things are possible with Thee, and Thou hast promised to give to them that ask. I most sincerely detest all the sins of my whole life; every fault, every imperfect inclination, which may be an obstacle to the graces which Thou desirest to bestow on Thy unworthy child. Vouchsafe, O my God, to purify my soul from every stain, by the infinite merits of the death and passion of Thy dear Son. I most sincerely resolve to serve Thee faithfully all the days of my life; but, of myself I am unable to do that which I desire and resolve to do; therefore, I beseech Thee to impart to me the graces of Thy Holy Spirit, that, like the Apostles, I may be endowed with strength from on high, and inspired with courage and resolution, to prove myself the disciple of Thy Son. I ardently desire to receive this most precious gift; but do Thou, O God, render my desire still stronger and more ardent, and accept, I beseech Thee, on my behalf, the fervent desire that animated the heart of the Blessed Virgin and the holy Apostles on the day of Pentecost, and let their perfect dispositions supply in all things my deficiencies, through Christ our Lord, Who, with Thee, in the unity of the Holy Ghost, ever liveth and reigneth God, world without end. Amen.

VENI CREATOR SPIRITUS!

Veni Creator Spiritus!
Mentes tuorum visita,
Imple superna gratia,
Quae Tu creasti pectora.

Come, Holy Ghost, Creator come,
From Thy bright heavenly throne!
Come, take possession of our souls,
And make them all Thine own!

Qui diceris Paraclitus,
Altissimi donum Dei,
Fons vivus, ignis, caritas,
Et spiritalis unctio.

Thou who art called the Paraclete,*
Best Gift of God above,
The Living Spring, the Living Fire,
Sweet Unction, and True Love!

Tu septiformis munere,
Digitus Paternae dexterae,
Tu rite promissum Patris,
Sermone ditans guttura.

Thou who art seven-fold in Thy grace,
Finger of God's right Hand,
His promise, teaching little ones
To speak and understand!

Accende lumen sensibus,
Infunde amorem cordibus,
Infirma nostri corporis
Virtute firmans perpeti.

O guide our minds with Thy blest light,
With love our hearts inflame,
And with Thy strength which ne'er
decays / Confirm our mortal frame.

Hostem repellas longius,
Pacemque dones protinus;
Ductore sic Te praevio
Vitemus omne noxium.

Far from us drive our hellish foe,
True peace unto us bring,
And through all perils guide us safe
Beneath Thy sacred wing.

* *Paraclete*: Defender, Comforter and Intercessor all in one.

Per Te sciamus da Patrem,	Through Thee may we the Father know,
Noscamus atque Filium,	Through Thee the Eternal Son,
Teque utriusque Spiritum,	And Thee the Spirit of them Both
Credamus omni tempore.	Thrice-blessed Three in One.
Deo Patri sit gloria,	All glory to the Father be,
Et Filio, qui a mortuis	And to the risen Son;
Surrexit, ac Paraclito,	The same to Thee, O Paraclete,
In saeculorum saecula.	While endless ages run.
Amen.	Amen.

II. THE RITE OF CONFIRMATION

The bishop, wearing over his rochet an amice, stole and cope of white color, and having a mitre on his head, proceeds to the faldstool before the middle of the altar, or has it placed for him in some other convenient place, and sits thereon, with his back to the altar and his face toward the people, holding his crosier in his left hand. He washes his hands, still sitting; then laying aside his mitre, he arises and standing with his face toward the persons to be confirmed, and having his hands joined before his breast (the persons to be confirmed kneeling and having their hands also joined before their breasts), he says:

May the Holy Ghost descend upon you, and may the power of the Most High preserve you from sin.

R. Amen.

Then, signing himself with the sign of the Cross, from his forehead to his breast, he says:

V. Our help is in the Name of the Lord.

R. Who hath made heaven and earth.

V. O Lord, hear my prayer.

R. And let my cry come unto Thee.

V. The Lord be with you.

R. And with thy spirit.

Then, with hands extended toward those to be confirmed, he says:

Let us pray,

Almighty and Eternal God, Who has vouchsafed to regenerate these Thy servants by water and the Holy Ghost, and hast given unto them forgiveness of all their sins: send forth from heaven upon them Thy sevenfold Spirit, the Holy Comforter.

R. Amen.

V. The Spirit of Wisdom and Understanding.

R. Amen.

V. The Spirit of Counsel and Fortitude.

R. Amen.

V. The Spirit of Knowledge and Piety.

R. Amen.

Fill them with the Spirit of Thy Fear, and sign them with the sign of the Cross ✠ of Christ, in Thy mercy, unto life eternal. Through the same our Lord Jesus Christ, Thy Son, Who liveth and reigneth with Thee in the unity of the same Holy Ghost, God, world without end.

R. Amen.

The bishop, sitting on the faldstool, or, if the number of persons to be confirmed requires it, standing, with his mitre on his head, confirms them, arranged in rows and kneeling in order. He inquires separately the name of each person to be confirmed, who is presented to him by the godfather or godmother, kneeling; and having dipped the end of the thumb of his right hand in chrism, he says:

I sign thee with the sign of the Cross. ✠

Whilst saying these words he makes the sign of the Cross with his thumb on the forehead of the person to be confirmed and then says:

And I confirm thee with the chrism of salvation. In the Name of he Father ✠ and of the Son ✠ and of the Holy ✠ Ghost.

R. Amen.

Then he strikes him gently on the cheek, saying:

Peace be with thee.

When all have been confirmed, the bishop wipes his hands with bread crumbs, and washes them over a basin. In the meantime the following antiphon is sung or read by the clergy:

Confirm, O God, that which Thou hast wrought in us, from Thy holy temple which is in Jerusalem.

V. Glory be to the Father, etc.

Then the antiphon "Confirm, O God" is repeated; after which the bishop, laying aside his mitre, rises up and standing toward the altar with his hands joined before his breast, says:

V. O Lord show Thy mercy upon us.

R. And grant us Thy salvation.

V. O Lord, hear my prayer.

R. And let my cry come unto Thee.

V. The Lord be with you.

R. And with thy spirit.

Then, with his hands still joined before his breast, and all the persons confirmed devoutly kneeling, he says:

O God, Who didst give to Thine Apostles the Holy Ghost, and didst ordain that by them and their successors He should be given to the rest of the faithful; look mercifully upon our unworthy service; and grant that the hearts of those whose foreheads we have anointed with holy chrism, and signed with the sign of the Holy Cross, may, by the same Holy Spirit, coming down upon them, and graciously abiding within them, be made the temple of His glory. Who, with the Father and the same Holy Ghost, livest and reignest, God, world without end.

R. Amen.

Then he says:

Behold, thus shall every man be blessed that feareth the Lord.

And, turning to the persons confirmed, he makes over them the sign of the Cross, saying:

May the Lord ✠ bless you out of Sion, that you may see the good things of Jerusalem all the days of your life, and may have life everlasting.

R. Amen.